The Usborne
Little Book
of
Animals

Paul Dowswell

Designed by Karen Tomlins
and Verinder Bhachu

Digital imaging: Fiona Johnson
Managing editor: Judy Tatchell
Consultant: Margaret Rostron

Using Internet links

Throughout this book we have suggested interesting websites where you can find out more about animals. To visit the sites, go to the Usborne Quicklinks Website at **www.usborne-quicklinks.com** and type the keywords "little animals". Here are some of the things you can do on the websites:

- Watch videos of baby animals
- Listen to exotic birds and reptiles
- Look at amazing close-up images of insects and other creepy-crawlies
- Explore a coral reef or visit a virtual zoo
- Find fun facts about many animals

Internet safety

When using the Internet, please make sure you follow these guidelines:

- Ask your parent's or guardian's permission before you connect to the Internet.
- If you write a message in a website guest book or on a website message board, do not include any personal information such as your full name, address or telephone number, and ask an adult before you give your email address.
- Never arrange to meet anyone you have talked to on the Internet.
- If a website asks you to log in or register by typing your name or email address, ask permission from an adult first.
- If you do receive an email from someone you don't know, tell an adult and do not reply to the email.

Computer not essential

If you don't have access to the Internet, don't worry. This book is a complete, self-contained reference book on its own.

Site availability

The links in Usborne Quicklinks are regularly reviewed and updated, but occasionally, you may get a message that a site is unavailable. This might be temporary, so try again later, or even the next day. Websites do occasionally close down and when this happens, we will replace them with new links in Usborne Quicklinks. Sometimes we add extra links too, if we think they are useful. So when you visit Usborne Quicklinks, the links may be slightly different from those described in your book.

Downloadable pictures

Pictures in this book marked with a ★ symbol can be downloaded from Usborne Quicklinks for your own personal use, for example, to illustrate a homework report or project. The pictures are the copyright of Usborne Publishing and may not be used for any commercial or profit-related purpose. To download a picture, go to Usborne Quicklinks and follow the instructions there.

Notes for parents and guardians

The websites described in this book are regularly reviewed and the links in Usborne Quicklinks are updated. However, the content of a website may change at any time and Usborne Publishing is not responsible for the content on any website other than its own. We recommend that children are supervised while on the Internet, that they do not use Internet chat rooms, and that you use Internet filtering software to block unsuitable material. Please ensure that your children read and follow the safety guidelines printed on the left. For more information, see the "Net Help" area on the Usborne Quicklinks Website.

To go to all the websites described in this book, go to **www.usborne-quicklinks.com** and enter the keywords "little animals".

Contents

This is a tree frog.
Like all frogs, it
has moist, slimy skin.

Animal world

There are millions of different animals, from tiny bugs to huge whales. Here are some of the different types of animals you can find out about in this book.

This Arctic tern's shape helps it to fly.

Mammals

Mammals feed their babies milk. Almost all have hair or fur, and most are lively and curious. From polar bears to camels, mammals can be found all over the world.

Like all baby mammals, this lion cub is taken care of by its mother.

Birds

Birds are the only animals that have feathers. They all have wings, but not all of them can fly. Some are powerful runners or swimmers. All birds lay eggs, and take care of their babies.

Reptiles

Reptiles have dry, scaly skin and almost all lay eggs. You can find reptiles in most countries, especially in the warmer parts of the world.

This reptile is a type of African lizard called an agama. It has tough, dry skin, and spikes along its back.

Amphibians

Amphibians are animals with soft, damp skin. They can breathe on land or in water. An amphibian needs to keep its body moist to stay alive, even if it lives on land.

Frogs are amphibians. They are excellent swimmers and can breathe underwater.

Creepy-crawlies

The world is teeming with creepy-crawlies such as insects, spiders, centipedes and snails. The most common creepy-crawlies are insects. They all have six legs, and most have wings. There are nearly two million different types of insects.

Like most insects, this wasp can fly.

Water life

Many different animals live in water – from fish to mammals such as dolphins and seals, and creatures such as jellyfish and lobsters. Some animals are even able to live in the deepest ocean.

Sea anemones and fish are just two of the many types of animals that live in water.

Internet link
For a link to a website where you can explore the wonderful world of animals, go to
www.usborne-quicklinks.com

Mammals

The animals on these two pages look different, but they are all mammals. There are more than four thousand different kinds of mammals, including you – humans are mammals, too.

Chimpanzees live in the forests of Africa.

Keeping warm

A mammal's body makes its own warmth and it can keep its temperature the same whether the day is hot or cold. This is called being warm-blooded.

The fur on this chimp helps to keep its body warm when the weather is cold.

Food for baby

All mammal mothers feed their babies milk. They make the milk in glands, called mammary glands, on their chests or bellies. Milk is a rich food but it is easy for a baby to swallow.

This baby deer is sucking milk from nipples on its mother's belly.

Flying mammal

Bats are the only mammals that can fly. Their wings are made of flaps of skin, which stretch over the bones of their arms and fingers

Fruit bat

Here you can see how a bat uses its arm as a wing. Long fingers support the wing skin.

★

Internet link

For a link to a website with lots of facts about mammals, go to **www.usborne-quicklinks.com**

Swimmers

Some mammals, such as whales, live in the sea. Like all mammals, they breathe air, so they come to the surface regularly.

Humpback whale ★

Whales are the biggest animals in the world.

Egg layers

A few mammals lay eggs, rather than give birth. One is the duck-billed platypus. It lays its eggs in a nest in a riverbank burrow.

★

Duck-billed platypus

What's for dinner?

Some animals eat plants, some eat meat, and some eat both. Plant-eaters have flat teeth to help them chew their food. Meat-eaters have sharp teeth to kill and eat their food.

Plant food

Many plant-eaters eat only one sort of plant, or just one part of a plant. Because of this, different plant-eaters can live in the same area and all have enough food. Here is an example of this, in the African grassland:

A gerenuk reaching for a leaf

Internet links

For links to websites where you can find lots of information about cheetahs and meet some real pandas, go to **www.usborne-quicklinks.com**

Bamboo eater

Living on only one kind of food can be risky. A giant panda eats huge amounts of bamboo. In some years the bamboo grows poorly, and many pandas starve.

Zebras graze on the grass.

Rhinos nibble at the bushes.

Giraffes eat tree-top leaves.

Gnawing teeth

Rats eat almost anything and can even gnaw through metal. They are a type of mammal called a rodent. All rodents have strong front teeth which never stop growing, and are worn down when they eat.

Rat

This panda is eating a bamboo shoot.

Meat-eater

Meat gives an animal more energy than plants, so meat-eaters, such as this lioness, spend less time eating than plant-eaters.

A lioness's jaws are packed with powerful muscles to help her kill and eat her prey.

Chaser

All big cats creep up on their prey, then rush out and grab it. Cheetahs do this too, but are also able to chase their victims over long distances. The chase makes them tired, but the meat they eat gives them back their energy.

A cheetah running at full speed. It can run at 115kph (70mph).

The lioness has different-shaped teeth to let her grip, tear and slice her food.

Night mammals

Huge numbers of animals,
including half of all types of
mammals, come out at night.
Many are meat-eaters
that feed on other
night animals.

Internet links

For links to websites where
you can meet many different
night animals and learn some
fun and friendly bat facts, go to
www.usborne-quicklinks.com

Night sight

Many animals that
hunt at night have
good eyesight to help
them find food.

Some have a special
layer at the back of
their eyes called a
tapetum. This helps
them pick up every
little glimmer of light
so they can see better
in the dark.

★

You can see the tapetum
glowing at the back of an
animal's eye, if it is caught
in a bright light.

Notice
how big the
tarsier's eyes
are compared
with its body.

Night animals
usually have
bigger eyes than
day animals. Big
eyes pick up much
more light.

This
tarsier
is out
hunting.
It eats
insects,
lizards, and
small bats.

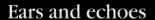

Ears and echoes

Most night animals have good hearing and big ears. This helps them pick up any noise which may lead them to food.

Bats hunt at night, and squeak as they fly. The sound of the squeak bounces off other animals, and comes back to the bat as an echo. The echo tells the bat where the animal is.

A bat sends out squeaks as it flies around.

The sound bounces off a nearby insect as an echo.

This leaf-nosed bat is hunting at night. Its big ears help it pick up every little sound.

Unusually for night animals, bats have small eyes and poor eyesight. Their hearing makes up for this.

Cool time

A lot of desert animals only come out in the cool of the night. It is too hot to hunt in the day.

This kangaroo rat leaves its den when the Sun goes down.

Food sniffer

Badgers have poor eyesight, but their sense of smell is superb. They have good hearing too.

Badgers sniff on the ground for food with their sensitive noses.

Hide-and-seek

Many animals have colors and patterns on their bodies to help them blend in with their surroundings. This is called camouflage. It can help them hunt without being seen, and makes it easier for the animals to hide from their enemies.

Internet link

For a link to a website that shows you how to hide, go to **www.usborne-quicklinks.com**

Stripes and spots

A lot of mammals that live in jungles or forests have stripes or spots on their fur. These match the patterns made by sunlight as it streams through the trees.

The stripes on this Indian tiger help it to blend into the long grass.

Most animals see in black and white, so a leopard in a tree is hard for them to see.

Plain coats

Dull colors can also provide camouflage. These gazelles blend in with dry, brown grassland.

Green fur

This three-toed sloth lives in the rainforest. Its gray fur is covered in tiny green plants. These colors help it hide from its enemies among the leaves.

Three-toed sloth

Gazelles leap high in the air to show enemies they are difficult to catch.

Gazelles' pale bellies and darker backs make them harder to see from a distance in the grassland.

Hazy stripes

Zebras have a strong pattern on their coats. But from a distance, the hazy heat on the African plains blurs the zebra's shape, and the stripes make it harder to see.

Changing seasons

By changing color with the seasons, animals such as mountain hares and arctic foxes stay camouflaged. Their fur is white in winter, but brown in summer, to match the plants and rocks.

A mountain hare's white coat matches the winter snow.

An arctic fox during the winter

An arctic fox during the summer

Escaping from enemies

Only the strongest, fiercest and biggest animals have no fear of being attacked by enemies. Most animals in the wild live in constant danger of being eaten. Here you can see some of the ways in which they protect themselves.

A squirrel has sharp claws to help it grip branches on the trees it climbs.

Up and away

Running away is often the best defense. Squirrels escape by climbing trees. They are very nimble and can leap onto very thin branches where their enemies cannot follow.

Internet link

For a link to a website that tells you how some animals escape from their enemies, go to **www.usborne-quicklinks.com**

Spikes for protection

The sharp spines on the back of a spiny anteater help protect it from enemies. Below you can see one of the ways in which it defends itself.

If an anteater is threatened, it begins to dig down.

It burrows down into the earth using its long claws.

Spines will cut the enemy's paws if it tries to dig it out.

A nasty smell

If a skunk is threatened, it turns its tail toward the enemy. It has a gland there which can squirt out a smelly liquid. The stink is so horrible that most enemies will leave it alone.

A skunk raises its tail when it is ready to squirt.

This is an addax. Its horns get bigger as it grows older.

Horned beasts

Some plant-eating animals have sharp horns on their head. Many use these to protect themselves from meat-eating enemies. The males also use the horns in fights with other males when they are competing to mate with females.

Horns are made of bone, with an outer layer of hard, fingernail-like tissue.

Scaly armor

Armadillos have horny, tough plates which protect them like a suit of armor. The plates stretch from the tip of their nose to the end of their tail. Each plate is linked to the next, so the armadillo is completely protected.

When an armadillo is attacked, it rolls into a tight ball.

Living together

Many mammals live in groups, rather than by themselves. This is because living in a group is safer, even for fierce hunters.

Prairie dogs live in groups in the grasslands of North America.

★

Zebra groups

Zebras live in small family groups made up of a male, several females, and their young. The group stays together as part of a larger herd.

★

Zebras in the same family nuzzle each other.

Family ties

Prairie dogs live in burrows in large family groups. When they meet, they sniff each other, like the two shown above. The smell tells one prairie dog whether the other is a member of its family.

These zebras are part of a large herd. There may be several hundred zebras in a herd.

The zebras below are looking out for enemies while the rest of the herd feeds.

Life with the lions

Lions are the only cats that live in groups. They survive by working closely with each other.

The male lions guard the group's territory. The lionesses hunt in small teams, setting up ambushes and diversions. They also look after the cubs.

A group of lions is called a pride.

Swingers

Gibbons live in families. A male and female mate for life and have a baby every two or three years.

The young stay with their parents for up to six years. Each family member searches for food on its own, but they keep in touch in the dense jungle by calling to each other.

A pair of gibbons

Baby mammals

Most newborn baby mammals are helpless and need a lot of care. Animals that can hide their young in a safe place, such as a nest, often have several babies. Animals that cannot do this usually have only one or two so they can guard them carefully.

Giraffe baby

Giraffes usually have only one baby at a time. A baby giraffe is an easy target for a lion. If an enemy comes near, the mother can kick it with her powerful legs.

Many babies

Mice have many babies at a time – eight is quite usual. The babies are born in a nest which keeps them warm. Many young are still caught by hunters such as owls and cats.

This giraffe mother licks her baby to clean it, so its scent does not attract an enemy.

Baby mice stay with their mother for less than a month.

★

Learning to hunt

Polar bear cubs spend two to three years with their mother, learning how to survive. The mother teaches them how to hunt. They leave her when they are old enough to hunt alone.

★

Baby polar bears stay close to their mother.

Pouch home

Marsupial mammals, like this kangaroo, carry their babies around in a built-in pouch. The baby feeds on milk from a nipple in the pouch. It also goes into the pouch if it is frightened or needs to rest.

★

A baby kangaroo can travel this way until it is a year old.

Internet link ✎

For a link to a website where you can watch videos of baby animals, go to **www.usborne-quicklinks.com**

Long childhood

Elephants take care of their babies for longer than any other animals except humans. A young elephant stays with its mother for up to ten years.

This baby elephant is learning to use its trunk to drink and bathe.

Sea mammals

Some mammals spend all their lives at sea. Others live near the shore, and spend some of the time on the beach.

A life at sea

There are three types of mammals that never come ashore – dolphins, whales and sea cows. All of these animals have flippers and a tail fin.

Whales

Whales are the biggest animals on Earth. They have a layer of fat under their skin called blubber, to help keep them warm.

Huge humpback whales like this one can be found in seas throughout the world.

★

A whale breathes through a blow-hole in its head. Stale air is blown out with a noisy snort.

Sea grazer

The animal on the right is called a sea cow, because it grazes on sea grasses and other underwater plants. It has a split upper lip to help it grasp its food.

★

Sea cows are gentle, placid creatures.

In and out

Seals, sea lions and walruses are sea mammals that spend part of their lives on land. They have flipper-like back legs, instead of a tail fin.

Seals are wonderful swimmers, but clumsy on land.

Dolphins

Dolphins are clever and friendly animals. They are also very fast swimmers. Like whales and sea cows, they wave their tail fins up and down to push themselves through the water.

Life on land

The main reason seals, sea lions and walruses come out of the sea is to mate and give birth. Below you can see how a ringed seal makes a den for its baby in the snow.

This female seal is looking for a gap in the ice. She will squeeze through to the snow above and begin to make her den.

She makes a hollow in the dense snow. When she has finished, her baby will have a safe and cozy shelter.

The baby seal, called a pup, spends six weeks in the den.

These are Atlantic spotted dolphins. Like all dolphins, they prefer to travel around in groups.

21

Bird life

Birds are the only animals that have feathers. Not all birds fly, but those that can't are usually superb swimmers or runners.

Fit for flying

Many birds are excellent fliers. Most of their bones are hollow, so they are light. Strong chest muscles power birds' wings. The sleek shape of their bodies helps them move quickly through the air.

A goose coming in to land lowers its feet, and spreads out its wings to slow down.

Body shapes

Birds have different body shapes. A goose's sturdy, muscular body is ideal for making long flights to warmer countries in winter. A kingfisher's arrow-like body lets it dart in and out of the water as it hunts.

A kingfisher uses its long, sharp beak to spear fish.

★

Internet link

For a link to a website where you can see pictures and facts about feathers, go to **www.usborne-quicklinks.com**

Types of feathers

Birds have three different kinds of feathers. Fluffy feathers, called down, keep them warm. Short, sturdy body feathers keep them dry. Long flight feathers help them take off, fly and land.

You can see this eagle's flight feathers on its wings.

Long flights

Birds are the greatest travelers in the animal world. Half of all types fly long distances to places where there is lots of food or where they can have babies. This is called migration.

★

In winter, these geese fly from Canada to Mexico in search of food.

This baby bird has a down coat to keep it warm in its cliff-top nest.

Feather growth

Baby birds are covered in down feathers. They grow body and flight feathers when they are older. All feathers get dirty and untidy. Birds clean and smooth them down with their beaks to keep them working properly.

This heron is cleaning its feathers.

★

Colors

Birds have all sorts of colors. Some have dull colors to help them hide in their surroundings. Others have bright, vivid colors to help other birds recognize them.

Pretty pink

Flamingos get their color from the pink shrimp and other small animals that they eat. If they did not eat this food, they would be a dull yellowy-brown.

A flamingo bending to feed in the water

Bright birds

Most parrots are beautiful colors. Their bright feathers stand out against the green forests where they live, and help other parrots find them.

This red-capped parrot lives in the forests of Western Australia.

Attracting females

Many male birds have bright colors to help them attract a mate. Females, in contrast, often look much duller.

These two brightly colored male pheasants use their vivid feathers to try to impress a female.

Lady Amherst's pheasant (male)

Chinese monal pheasant (male)

Bright bills

At mating time, male and female tufted puffins grow colorful feathers at the back of their head. Their beaks also become much brighter and grow an extra layer. Later, the new layer drops off.

Before puffins mate, they rub their bright beaks together.

Internet links

For links to websites with flamingo videos and sounds and that show you an island where puffins live, go to **www.usborne-quicklinks.com**

Hiding away

Many birds have colors which help them hide from their enemies. In winter, a ptarmigan has white feathers to match the snow. When the snow melts, the feathers turn browner, to match the surroundings. Most baby birds have dull-colored feathers, too.

Almost all baby birds have camouflage colors to keep them hidden from hunters.

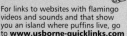

Ptarmigan

25

In the air

All birds have wings, even those that can't fly. Being able to fly lets a bird catch food in the air, or travel to warmer places to build a nest and find food. Flying also helps birds to escape from their enemies.

Internet links

For links to websites where you can find helpful information about birds and flight, go to **www.usborne-quicklinks.com**

A stork stretches into a streamlined shape to fly through the air. This one is carrying branches for its nest.

Taking off

Not all birds take off in the same way. Small birds can just jump into the air, but large birds, such as swans, have to work a lot harder to get airborne.

A swan stretches out its wings.

It flaps and runs along the water.

It launches itself into the air.

26

Big and small flyers

Small birds beat their wings quickly to stay in the air. Most have short wings that are ideal for darting through trees and branches. Most big birds have large wings. They glide to save energy, only beating their wings now and then.

Because birds have hollow bones, even big ones are usually light enough to fly.

When a tiny hummingbird beats its wings very fast, it can hover in the air.

Birds that can't fly

Ostriches are the biggest birds in the world. They are too heavy for their little wings to carry them into the air. Instead, they have huge, powerful legs and run very fast.

Ostriches running

Penguins can't fly, but they can swim underwater, and use their wings like flippers. They are very graceful swimmers, and move very quickly.

Penguins dive underwater to hunt for fish.

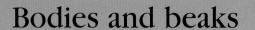

Bodies and beaks

The shape of a bird's body and beak help it to find and eat the kind of food it likes. You can see here that there are huge differences in body and beak shapes.

Sea life

Puffins live by the sea and hunt fish. Their stubby, muscular bodies and short wings help them swim well underwater. They can fly, but they are much clumsier in the air than in the sea.

Wings and claws

This bald eagle's huge wings let it glide effortlessly over water as it searches for fish. Its sharp claws hold fish tightly as it returns to its nest to feed.

This bald eagle has sharp claws for grasping fish.

This is a puffin. Its webbed feet help it paddle in the sea.

Beak shapes

Birds use their beaks as tools to help them find food. This toucan's long beak lets it reach for fruit among dense forest branches.

The toucan's jagged beak helps it to grip fruit firmly.

Diggers

Like many river and seashore birds, the scarlet ibis has a long, thin beak. It uses it to poke around for small shrimp and worms at the muddy edges of rivers.

Scarlet ibis

Spears and nets

Many birds eat other animals. Some are fierce hunters that can kill animals as big as a monkey. Here are three flesh-eating birds that use their beaks in different ways.

★ A heron uses its dagger-like beak to spear fish.

★ A vulture's hooked beak lets it tear meat from a dead animal.

★ A pelican uses its sack-shaped beak like a fishing net.

Internet link

For a link to a website with lots of information about birds' beaks and feet, go to **www.usborne-quicklinks.com**

Nests and chicks

Once she has laid her eggs, a female bird needs to sit on them to keep them warm. If the eggs get too cold, the babies inside will die.

A safe spot

Most birds build nests to protect the mother and her eggs from enemies. Nests also make a safe place for the babies when they hatch.

Internet link

For a link to a website with an online game about different kinds of nests, go to **www.usborne-quicklinks.com**

Types of nests

Each type of bird has its own way of building a nest. Many are cup-shaped, and made of mud, hair, feathers and twigs.

A swallow's nest is made of mud and stuck to a wall.

A tailor bird sews big leaves together with plant parts.

A long-tailed tit makes a nest of moss, lichen and cobwebs.

This Eurasian tit's nest is made of twigs and reeds.

30

Breaking out

Birds sit on their eggs for two weeks or more. (Bigger birds sit for longer.) When the baby is ready to hatch, it chips its way out of the egg. Most bird babies need a lot of looking after.

This baby moorhen is chipping its way out of its egg.

A hoopoe feeding a hungry chick

Hungry babies

Baby birds are always hungry, and need a constant supply of food. An adult hoopoe, for example, must make hundreds of journeys to and from its nest every day. It brings insects and grubs for its chicks.

Protecting the family

Swans build large waterside nests from plant stalks. Their babies (called cygnets) stay with them for around four months. The parents protect their young and take them to feeding places. When the cygnets leave, they live alone until they find a mate.

This mother swan and her cygnets are gathered around their nest.

Reptile life

What makes a reptile a reptile? It has scaly skin, it lays eggs and it is "cold-blooded". This means its body does not make heat and is as warm or as cold as the air around it. Lizards, snakes, turtles and crocodiles are all reptiles.

This snake is a tree python. It hunts birds.

Snakes

All snakes are meat-eaters. Some eat insects and worms. Some can eat animals as big as a crocodile. You can find snakes all over the world, except in Antarctica.

Internet link

For a link to a website where you can find reptile facts, videos, pictures and games, go to **www.usborne-quicklinks.com**

Lizards

Most lizards are small, nimble creatures, although a few can grow to be as much as 3m (10ft) long. Like snakes, they can be found almost everywhere on Earth.

Crocodiles

Crocodiles, and their close relatives, alligators, are fierce hunters. They can be found on riverbanks in hot countries. In the right conditions, crocodiles can live for over 100 years.

This calotes lizard lives in the forests of southern India.

Its long tail helps the calotes balance on thin branches.

Nile crocodile

Hawksbill
turtle ★

Turtles

Turtles spend
their lives in warm,
shallow seas, and only
ever come onto land to
lay eggs. Some swim very
long distances to find a
place to have babies.

Tortoises

Tortoises are similar
to turtles, but they
live on land instead
of water.

Tortoises are well
protected by their
hard outer
shells.

★

Hot and cold

As reptiles are cold-blooded,
heat and cold affect them
more than warm-blooded
animals. If they are too
cold, they become
sluggish. If they are too
hot, they dry up and
die. A reptile spends a
lot of the day trying
to stay at the right
temperature.

This iguana's
leathery skin
helps prevent it
from drying up.

Morning. Sits in
sun to warm up
after cool night.

Noon. Hides in
shade at hottest
time of day.

Afternoon. Moves in
and out of sun, to
keep warm or cool.

Snap and grab

Most reptiles are meat-eaters. They often catch their prey in extraordinary ways.

Shooter

A chameleon eats insects. When it gets near its prey, it wraps its tail around a branch. Then it takes careful aim and shoots out its long, sticky tongue. It needs to be silent, fast and accurate, because insects move so fast.

Internet links

For links to websites where you can find out about poisonous snakes and learn to speak "crocodilian", go to **www.usborne-quicklinks.com**

Deadly surprise

Crocodiles lurk just below the surface of a river. They spring out and catch an animal drinking at the water's edge. A crocodile cannot chew, so it swallows small prey whole. It uses its powerful jaws to bite and crush larger prey before it swallows them.

This chameleon is ready to strike. It stays very still, so the insect does not notice it.

It shoots out its long tongue, which is curled up in its mouth.

The insect sticks to the tongue. It is pulled in and eaten.

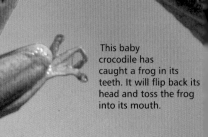

This baby crocodile has caught a frog in its teeth. It will flip back its head and toss the frog into its mouth.

Snake table manners

Snakes have several fascinating and revolting ways of killing their food. Many can eat animals that are much bigger than themselves.

A snake can separate its upper and lower jaws. This lets it open its mouth very wide. Its body also stretches to hold the food it is eating.

The boomslang snake climbs trees and snatches birds from their nests.

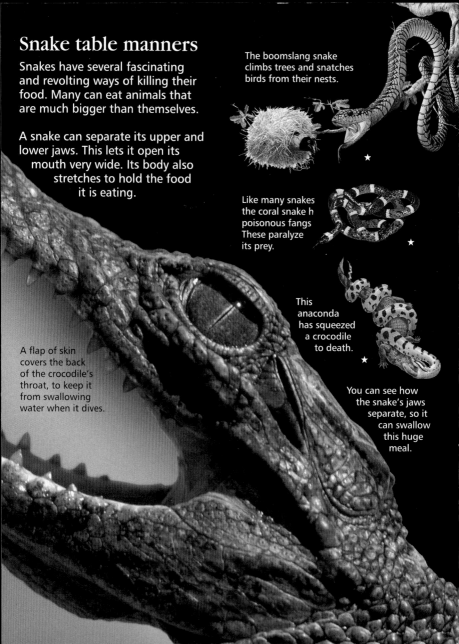

Like many snakes the coral snake h poisonous fangs These paralyze its prey.

This anaconda has squeezed a crocodile to death.

A flap of skin covers the back of the crocodile's throat, to keep it from swallowing water when it dives.

You can see how the snake's jaws separate, so it can swallow this huge meal.

Special senses

Reptiles sense the world in the same way as other animals – with taste, smell, sight, hearing and touch. But some reptiles make use of these senses in unusual ways.

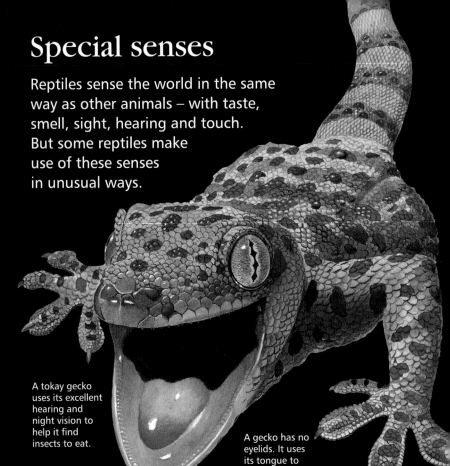

A tokay gecko uses its excellent hearing and night vision to help it find insects to eat.

A gecko has no eyelids. It uses its tongue to clean its eyes.

Night sight

Like many night hunters, the tokay gecko has big eyes to help it to take in a lot of light. During the day its pupils close up to a little slit to protect its super-sensitive eyes from bright light.

The pupil gets very small during the day, and lets in very little light.

The pupil opens wide at night, to let in as much light as possible.

"Seeing" heat

Many reptiles have extra senses. A pit viper, for instance, can "see" heat. Two little pits on either side of its head detect tiny amounts of heat given out by other animals' bodies. This extra sense lets it hunt in the dark.

The pit viper's pits are just in front of its eyes.

Cross-eyed

A chameleon's eyes can look in two directions at once. They swivel around in search of insects. No one knows if its brain sees one or two pictures at a time.

Notice how this chameleon's eyes are looking in different directions.

This eyelash viper is "tasting" the air with its tongue.

Forked tongue

Snakes have very poor eyesight and hearing. Most find their prey by smell and by feeling the vibrations through the ground caused by an animal's movements. They can also pick up the scent of other animals by "tasting" the air with their forked tongue.

Internet links

For links to websites where you can find out how a snake's senses help it to hunt, and discover fascinating facts about animals and their different senses, go to
www.usborne-quicklinks.com

Reptile defenses

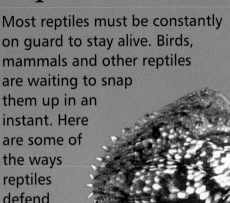

Most reptiles must be constantly on guard to stay alive. Birds, mammals and other reptiles are waiting to snap them up in an instant. Here are some of the ways reptiles defend themselves.

This frilled lizard is trying to look frightening.

Getting bigger

Some reptiles make themselves look bigger and fiercer when cornered by an enemy. Most do this by spreading out part of their body. This frilled lizard stretches out a frill of skin around its neck and hisses loudly. If this doesn't work, it runs away.

> **Internet link**
>
> For a link to a website where you can see how lizards defend themselves, go to **www.usborne-quicklinks.com**

Color change

A chameleon can change the color of its skin to blend with its surroundings. Its color also shows its mood. Below, you can see how it changes color.

The chameleon has turned bright green to match the leaves.

Now it has turned light brown to match the forest floor.

It turns striped to warn an enemy when it is angry.

This chameleon is hiding in a tree.

Spikes

The moloch's body is covered with spikes as sharp as thorns. This makes it very unpleasant to chew.

This is a moloch. It is also called a thorny devil.

Tail trick

A special trick can often fool an attacker. Most lizards can break off their tail if attacked. The tail wriggles for several minutes, distracting the attacker.

This skink lizard has shed its tail.

Playing dead

Many attackers only eat meat they have killed themselves. Some reptiles take advantage of this by pretending to be dead when threatened.

This ringed snake is pretending to be dead.

Young reptiles

Some reptile parents protect their eggs and their babies when they hatch. But most reptiles lay their eggs in a safe place and just leave the babies to fend for themselves.

Caring crocs

Nile crocodiles care for their babies. The mother lays 40 eggs, and both parents guard them for 90 days.

When the babies hatch, the mother gathers them in her mouth and takes them to a quiet pool to look after them.

A bad start

Turtles lay their eggs at night in burrows on the beach. The turtles then return to the sea. When the baby turtles hatch, they dash to the sea. The journey is very dangerous and many are eaten on the way by crabs and seabirds.

Baby turtles run as fast as they can, trying to reach the sea before they get eaten.

This is a baby crocodile hatching from an egg.

Here is a turtle laying her eggs in a burrow.

As it comes out of the egg, a baby crocodile makes little squeaking noises to attract its mother's attention.

Body nest

Snakes usually leave their eggs after laying them, but this python protects them by making a nest with her body. She lays about 100 eggs and coils around them for three months. The eggs need to be warm to develop, so the python shivers to raise her temperature by a few degrees.

Internet links

For links to websites with online activities about the leatherback sea turtle, and a video of baby turtles hatching, go to **www.usborne-quicklinks.com**

An Australian python. You can see the eggs within her coils.

Quick hatchers

Some reptiles give birth to live young, and others, such as the dwarf chameleon, lay eggs which hatch soon afterwards. Many animals eat other animals' eggs. Staying in an egg for a short time gives a baby reptile a greater chance of surviving.

A chameleon lays a sticky egg on a twig.

The egg has a fully developed baby inside it.

After only a few hours, the baby hatches.

Miniature grown-ups

When reptiles hatch, they are fully developed and ready to face the world on their own. Although they are smaller than adults, they have all their parents' abilities and instincts.

A baby gecko, fresh from its egg

Amphibians

Amphibians look a little like reptiles, but with soft, moist skin. They lay squishy eggs in water, where their young hatch and grow. Adults can live on land and in water. Frogs and toads are amphibians.

Slimy skin

Many amphibians have shiny, slimy skin. They need to keep their skin moist, even when they are on land. If their skin becomes too dry, they may die.

This tree frog lives in rainforest trees. Moisture in the air helps to keep its skin damp.

Getting air

Amphibians are clever breathers. They can take in air through their skin on land and underwater. Some have gills, like fish (see page 54). On land, many amphibians breathe through their mouths.

The frilly growths on this axolotl's head are gills. It uses them to breathe underwater.

Swimming

An amphibian's body has special features that let it walk or swim. Frogs, for instance, have webbed toes. They use these like flippers to push themselves through the water.

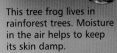

★

Webbed toes

Frogs and toads

Frogs have long, strong back legs. They use them to leap around on land, and swim in water. Many frogs have beautiful, bright skin. Toads have drier, warty skin.

Internet link

For a link to a website where you can find lots of weird and wonderful facts about frogs and toads, as well as games, jokes and pictures, go to **www.usborne-quicklinks.com**

Toads have shorter back legs than frogs. They waddle rather than hop.

Toad

Frog

Salamanders

A salamander has a long tail like a lizard. Most salamanders have foul-tasting skin which is brightly patterned. This warns their enemies not to try eating them because they will taste horrible.

The pattern on this salamander warns its enemies that it tastes bad.

Babies

Many frogs and toads lay lots of eggs at once. When they hatch, the babies live in water. They don't look like their parents at all. When they grow up, they move onto land.

These squishy blobs are frogs' eggs, called spawn. The babies, called tadpoles, hatch out of them.

After a few weeks the tadpoles start to grow legs. The back legs grow first, then the front legs.

Eventually, the tail shrinks away and the tadpole grows lungs. It can now breathe on land.

It takes about 16 weeks for a tadpole to become a frog. It still has a lot of growing to do.

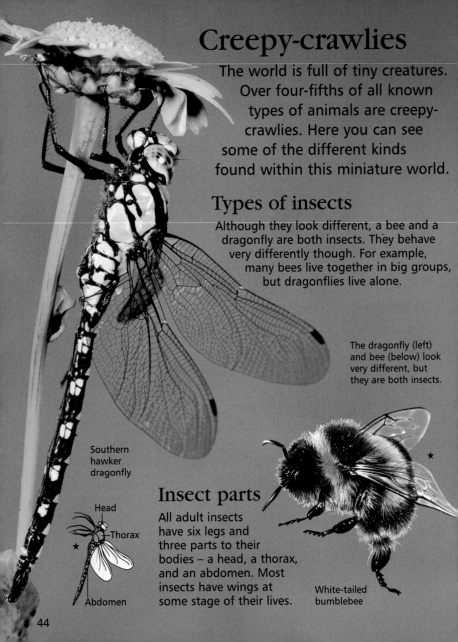

Creepy-crawlies

The world is full of tiny creatures. Over four-fifths of all known types of animals are creepy-crawlies. Here you can see some of the different kinds found within this miniature world.

Types of insects

Although they look different, a bee and a dragonfly are both insects. They behave very differently though. For example, many bees live together in big groups, but dragonflies live alone.

The dragonfly (left) and bee (below) look very different, but they are both insects.

Southern hawker dragonfly

Head

Thorax

★

Abdomen

Insect parts

All adult insects have six legs and three parts to their bodies – a head, a thorax, and an abdomen. Most insects have wings at some stage of their lives.

White-tailed bumblebee

Spiders

Spiders are not insects. They are a type of animal known as an arachnid. Spiders have eight legs and two parts to their body. They never have wings. Many spiders spin webs to catch their food.

The golden orb weaver is one of Australia's biggest spiders. Females can be 4.5cm (2in) long.

Internet link

For a link to a website where you can take a closer look at insects, go to **www.usborne-quicklinks.com**

Lots of legs

Millipedes and centipedes have the most legs of any animal. Centipedes have up to 100 legs, while some millipedes have up to 700. Their bodies are divided into a series of segments. Like many creepy-crawlies, they have feelers called antennae on their heads.

Two rainforest millipedes

Slimy snails

Snails have a hard shell they can curl up in. This protects their bodies from enemies. Land snails, such as the one on the right, lurk in damp places, such as under leaves and stones. Some snails can live underwater.

A snail can pull its whole body into its shell if it is in danger.

This is a kind of snail called a grove snail. Like all snails, it slides along on its slimy belly.

Baby bugs

Most female creepy-crawlies lay eggs. Some leave their eggs to hatch alone, others guard them. A few even look after their babies.

Parent care

Moths lay their eggs on leaves and then fly off. The babies that hatch are called caterpillars. They come out of their eggs with a huge appetite, but have a good supply of food all around them.

This moth caterpillar is eating a leaf.

A wolf spider takes her eggs wherever she goes. She spins a cocoon to carry them, and looks after them until they hatch.

A wolf spider carrying her eggs in a cocoon

Internet link

For a link to a website with facts about spiders and their babies, go to **www.usborne-quicklinks.com**

This female scorpion guards her eggs and then carries her babies around on her back.

A scorpion carrying her babies

Lookalikes

Some creepy-crawlies, such as snails and grasshoppers, have babies that look like small versions of themselves. A young snail's shell and skin grow as the snail grows.

Snail babies look just like miniature adults. Their shells grow as they get bigger.

A young grasshopper's skin does not grow. As the young animal gets bigger, a new, larger skin forms inside the old one. The old skin splits and the animal wriggles out.

You can see the old skin of the grasshopper's antennae.

This young grasshopper is wriggling out of its old skin.

The wings are still too small for the grasshopper to fly.

A big change

Some young creepy-crawlies look quite different from their parents. A ladybug's egg hatches into a grub called a larva. It grows, then makes a hard case around itself, called a pupa. Inside, it turns into an adult. After three weeks, the adult comes out. It is yellow but soon changes color.

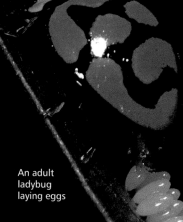

An adult ladybug laying eggs

Ladybug larva. It eats a lot and grows bigger.

Ladybug pupa. It is attached to a leaf.

New adult. It will soon turn black and red.

47

Bug food

Most creepy-crawlies eat only one kind of food. Many eat meat, but more than half feed on plants. Some even feed on the droppings of other animals. Here you can see some of the ways in which creepy-crawlies find, eat and store their food.

This ant has been stuffed full of honey by other ants in its colony. It stores the honey for when the colony is short of food.

Internet link

For a link to a website with amazing close-up pictures of insect mouth parts, go to **www.usborne-quicklinks.com**

Green crickets have powerful jaws. They cause a lot of damage to crops.

Mouth parts

An insect's mouth is designed to eat a certain kind of food. Below you can see three very different types of insect mouth parts.

A grasshopper has a pair of jaws that work like pliers. These nip off tiny pieces of plants.

A female mosquito has a long, sharp tube (shown in red). She uses it to pierce skin and suck blood.

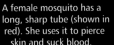

A fly has a mouth like a sponge to mop up its food.

Silky trap

Like many spiders, this orb spider spins a web to catch its food. The silky thread is made in a special pouch in the spider's abdomen.

This orb spider's web is sticky. Flies that land on it get stuck.

Web thread is made at the tip of the abdomen.

The spider's legs have an oily film on them, to keep them from sticking to the web.

Dung

Dung beetles eat the droppings of other animals. The couple below are taking some back to their burrow. The female will lay eggs in it, so their babies will have a supply of food when they hatch.

★

Dung beetles

Suckers

Some insects, such as the assassin bug, inject spit into their victims. The spit dissolves the victim from the inside. The assassin bug then sucks the juices out.

This assassin bug is attacking a ladybug.

★

Colors and tricks

Creepy-crawlies come in
all shapes and colors. Some
have features which can help to
trick or frighten an enemy. Others
have their own built-in weapons.

Tail
end

Real
head

★

Invisible killer

A flower mantis is lurking
on this bougainvillaea plant.
Its shape and color resemble
the surrounding flowers. When
another insect lands on the
plant, the mantis pounces.

This butterfly
has a false
head on its tail
end to confuse
enemies.

To another insect,
this flower mantis
looks like a flower.

Internet link

For a link to a website where you can try to spot some hidden insects, go to **www.usborne-quicklinks.com**

Watch it!

Some creepy-crawlies have alarming colors. The bright, shiny cases of these harlequin bugs can easily be seen against a leaf. The colors warn enemies that they taste bad.

Enemies soon learn to leave these harlequin bugs alone.

Blob warfare

A sawfly larva feeds on pine needles, which contain a sticky liquid called resin. If the larva is attacked, it can also use the resin as a weapon.

A sawfly larva is attacked by an ant.

It coughs up a blob of sticky resin.

The larva gums up the ant with the resin.

Stingers

Insects such as wasps and bees have a stinger in their tail. This injects chemicals which hurt or kill an opponent.

This sand wasp is paralyzing a caterpillar with its stinger.

Butterflies

Butterflies are among the most colorful types of insects. Most live for only a few weeks. They find a mate, lay eggs, then die.

Butterfly wings

Butterfly wings are covered in tiny colored, shiny scales. The shiny scales reflect light, which is why butterflies shimmer when they fly.

Butterflies visit plants to drink a liquid, called nectar, from flowers.

This butterfly is called a common blue. It has spread its wings to soak up the Sun's heat.

Open and shut

When a butterfly holds its wings open, it is gathering warmth from the Sun. This helps give it the energy to fly. When its wings are closed, it is resting. It faces the Sun, so its shadow is small and enemies are less likely to spot it.

Butterfly with wings open

Butterfly with wings closed

Internet link

For a link to a website where you can find many interesting butterfly facts, plus games and activities, go to **www.usborne-quicklinks.com**

Wing patterns

A butterfly's beautiful, patterned wings help other butterflies spot their own kind. Their wing patterns help butterflies in other ways, too.

A comma's ragged wings disguise it as a dead leaf when it is on the ground.

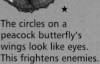

The circles on a peacock butterfly's wings look like eyes. This frightens enemies.

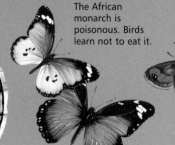

The African monarch is poisonous. Birds learn not to eat it.

An Arctic ringlet's dark wings help it soak up heat.

This mocker swallowtail is not poisonous, but birds think it is an African monarch and do not eat it.

The patterns on this tortoiseshell's wings help it attract a mate.

Making butterflies

A female butterfly lays her eggs on a plant. When an egg hatches, a caterpillar comes out and feeds on the plant. When the caterpillar is fully grown, it turns into a pupa, and then into a butterfly.

A caterpillar ready to turn into a pupa

The pupa forms inside the body. It splits the skin.

The pupa hardens. Inside, it is changing.

After two weeks a butterfly comes out.

The butterfly's body hardens and it flies off.

Living in the sea

The sea is full of life. Most sea creatures live around the coast, but you can also find them in the middle of the ocean, and on the deepest sea floor.

What is a fish?

All fish live in water. They have a skeleton inside their body, and most types are covered with small, smooth plates called scales.

Flexible fish

Sharks and rays are not like other fish. Their skeletons are made of bendable cartilage rather than bone, and they have rough scales.

This fish is a sweetlips. It has smooth scales on its body.

The scales on this ray feel like sandpaper.

Breathing

Fish "breathe" by pushing water over rows of feather-like gills at the back of their mouths. The gills take oxygen from the water.

The fish opens its mouth to take in water.

Water passes over gills and out of gill slit.

Other creatures

Not only fish live in the sea. From whales to starfish, there are as many different types of animals in the sea as there are on land. Here are some animals that all live by the shore.

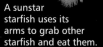

A sunstar starfish uses its arms to grab other starfish and eat them.

Slugs

This brightly colored sea slug is a relative of the much duller-looking land slug. Its bright colors are a warning to other animals that it is poisonous.

This sea slug has stinging tentacles.

Shell home

Most crabs are protected by a hard case which covers their body. The hermit crab, though, only has a case over its front half. To protect the rest, it backs into an empty seashell and carries this around.

Hermit crabs find an empty seashell to protect their back parts. Here you can see the borrowed shell.

Worms

Many kinds of worms live in the shallows at the edge of the sea. This green leaf worm can be found crawling in rock pools and wet sandy beaches.

★

Green leaf worm

Baby fish

Most fish lay eggs. Some lay up to 200,000 at once. Many eggs will be eaten by other creatures, but some grow to be adults. Only a few fish look after their eggs before they hatch. Fewer still look after their young after they have hatched.

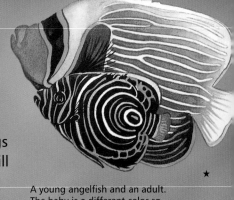

A young angelfish and an adult. The baby is a different color so the adult will not think it is a rival, and attack it.

This male seahorse is carrying eggs in its swollen belly.

Seahorses

When seahorses breed, the male seahorse carries the female's eggs in a pouch in his belly. The babies look just like tiny adults, and they swim off as soon as they come out of the pouch.

Here you can see a baby seahorse coming out of its father's pouch.

Mouth cradle

A cardinal fish keeps its eggs safe by hiding them in its mouth. It doesn't feed while carrying the eggs, which may take up to a month to hatch. If it is disturbed or frightened, it may swallow all the eggs.

The eggs in the cardinal fish's mouth look like tiny glass balls.

Egg to fry

Most fish eggs float in the water, or lie among weeds or rocks. The young fish that hatch are called fry. Here is how an egg changes to a baby:

★ This fish egg is filled with yolk. The baby inside the egg grows by feeding on the yolk.

★ The baby has hatched. It still lives on the yolk which it carries in a sac under its body.

★ The yolk lasts until the young fish is big enough to find other food for itself.

Safe spot

After hatching, a baby fish is still in danger of being eaten by an enemy. A type of freshwater fish called a cichlid not only keeps its eggs in its mouth, it keeps its young there until they are big enough to hunt for themselves.

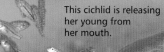

This cichlid is releasing her young from her mouth.

Internet link

For a link to a website where you can read more about seahorses, go to **www.usborne-quicklinks.com**

Sea hunters

Sea creatures eat what they can, when they can. Some may go without food for days. Others catch food all the time. Here are some of the ways they hunt.

Teeth and jaws

These three fish have different-shaped mouths. A basking shark swims around with its mouth open. It catches tiny animals in its throat.

A gulper eel lives in deep water where food is scarce. Its huge mouth helps it eat fish of almost any size.

A barracuda has sharp teeth in its powerful mouth. It can take a bite out of a much bigger fish, then quickly swim away.

Gulper eel

★

Basking shark

★

Barracuda

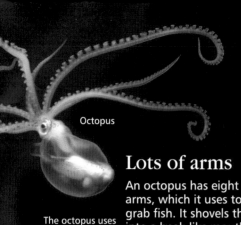

Octopus

A fishing fish

An angler fish has a small, wriggling "bait" attached to its head. It lures other fish with it.

This angler fish is lurking on the sea bed. It snaps up fish that come up to investigate.

★

Lots of arms

An octopus has eight arms, which it uses to grab fish. It shovels them into a beak-like mouth on the underside of its body.

The octopus uses rows of suckers on its arms to grip its prey.

Internet link
For a link to a website with information about many different sea creatures, go to **www.usborne-quicklinks.com**

Lionfish

Fin trap

A lionfish uses its long, spiny fins to steer small fish into the sides of the coral reef where it hunts. When the fish are cornered, the lionfish pounces.

Lionfish have very sharp, poisonous fins.

Sea monsters

The seas and oceans are patrolled by sharks – some of the fiercest hunters in the world. Creatures even more terrifying lurk within the depths of the ocean.

Rows of sharp teeth stick out of the shark's jaw.

Eating machines

Sharks have sharp, saw-edged teeth. These help them rip their food into pieces that are easy to swallow. The teeth often fall out, but new ones grow.

This sand tiger shark eats other fish. Three or four sand tigers will surround a group of fish and eat them all.

Cross section of a shark's lower jaw, showing teeth.

The shark loses a tooth when it bites a victim.

A new tooth moves forward to replace it.

Dark life

The deep sea is a bleak place to live. It is dark and very cold, and no plants live there. The few fish that can survive there are very good hunters. They have to catch whatever food they can find.

Internet link

For a link to a website where you can watch video clips of sharks, go to **www.usborne-quicklinks.com**

This deep-sea fish has teeth that point back, making it difficult for other fish to wriggle free.

Teeth and spots

Most deep-sea fish have a large mouth and very sharp teeth, to help them hold onto the food they grab. Many have glowing spots, which lure other fish to them.

This viper fish has luminous spots on its body.

Tiny fish

This small lantern fish feeds on shrimp. It often swims up to the top layer of the ocean to hunt.

This lantern fish is no bigger than a man's thumb.

On and off

Flashlight fish have a luminous bulge just below their eyes. They can turn it on and off. Scientists think they may do this to signal to one another.

This flashlight fish has its light on.

Coral reefs

Coral reefs grow close to the coast in warm seas. They are full of fish and other sea animals. There is plenty of food here, and the reef has many caves and crevices to hide in.

Coral home

Reefs are made of tiny creatures called corals. Their soft bodies are protected by a hard outer skeleton. New corals grow on top of the dead skeletons of other corals. Millions of dead and living corals make up a reef.

Many different corals live side by side on the reef.

Helping out

These blue and black cleaner fish are eating pests and dead skin on a big grouper fish. The cleaners get a free meal, and the grouper gets a good cleaning.

★

A small cleaner fish feeds quite safely inside a grouper's mouth.

Inflatable fish

A fantastic number of different animals live on a coral reef. The creature below is a puffer fish. It blows itself up into a spiky ball if it is in danger.

A puffer fish usually looks like this.

★

When a puffer fish is in danger, it swells up. Its spikes make it unpleasant to eat.

Coral nibbler

Parrot fish get their name from the bird-like beak they have for a mouth. They use it to nibble the hard coral, and eat the tiny soft creatures inside.

★

Parrot fish

Bright colors

The creature on the right is a kind of sea slug. Its bright colors warn other animals that it is poisonous. The sea slug waves the flaps on the sides of its body to swim.

The orangey, finger-like structures are the sea slug's gills.

Index of animal names

Acknowledgments

American editor: Carrie A. Seay **Digital illustrations:** Richard Cox **Additional design:** Jane Rigby

Photo credits key t – top, m – middle, b – bottom.

1 Digital Vision; 2–3 Digital Vision; 4–5 Digital Vision; 6 © Karl Ammann/karlammann.com; 7 © Jack Fields/CORBIS; 8 © M & C Denis-Huot/Still Pictures; 9 stevebloom.com; 10 © Ken Lucas/Ardea.com; 11 © Joe McDonald/CORBIS; 12 © Anup Shah/naturepl.com; 13 © Neil McIntyre; 14 © Roger Wilmshurst/flpa/CORBIS; 15 © Steve Kaufman/CORBIS; 16–17 © Frank Krahmer/Getty Images; 17 Digital Vision; 18 © Karl Ammann/CORBIS; 19 © Winifred Wisniewski/FLPA/CORBIS; 20–21 © Pete Atkinson/Getty Images; 22 (b) © Doc White/naturepl.com; 22 © George Lepp/CORBIS; 23 © Wolfgang Kaehler/CORBIS; 24 © John Cancalosi/Bruce Coleman Collection; 25 © Dr. Scott Neilson/Bruce Coleman Collection; 26–27 photolibrary.com/Oxford Scientific/© Brian Kenney; 27 © Joe McDonald/Bruce Coleman Collection; 29 © Michael Sewell/Still Pictures; 30 © Uwe Walz/CORBIS; 31 (tr) Digital Vision, (br) © Jonathan Smith/Cordaiy Photo/CORBIS; 32 (tl) photolibrary.com/Oxford Scientific/© Brian Kenney, (br) © K. Jayaram/Planet Earth Pictures; 33 © T. A. Vincent/Planet Earth Pictures; 34–35 © Jonathan Blair/CORBIS; 37 © Kevin Schafer/CORBIS; 38 © David A Northcott/CORBIS; 42–43 Digital Vision; 42 (tl) © Jane Burton/Warren Photographic; 43 (r) © Linda Richardson/CORBIS; 44 © Geoff du Feu/Getty Images; 45 © Mick Martin; 46 (l) © Karen Tweedy Holmes/CORBIS, (tr) © Andrew Purcell/Bruce Coleman Collection; 47 (t) photolibrary.com/Oxford Scientific/© Waina Cheng Ward, (bl) Digital Vision; 48 © Michael and Patricia Fogden/CORBIS; 49 © Anthony Bannister ABPL/CORBIS; 50 © Michael and Patricia Fogden/CORBIS; 51 © David Maitland/Getty Images; 54–55 © Corbis Lawson Wood/CORBIS; 55 (t) OAR/National Undersea Research Program (NURP), (b) © Nancy Sefton; 56 © J & B Speigel Waters/Planet Earth Pictures; 57 (t) © Peter Rowlands, (b) © Georgette Douwma; 58 © Stephen Frink/CORBIS; 59 (t) © Jeffrey Rotman/CORBIS, (b) © Stephen Frink/CORBIS; 60 © Jeffery Rotman/Still Pictures; 61 © Peter David/Natural Visions; 62 © Lawson Wood/CORBIS; 63 © Robert Yin/CORBIS.

Every effort has been made to trace and acknowledge ownership of copyright. The publishers will be glad to make suitable arrangements with any copyright holder whom it has not been possible to contact.

Illustrator credits

Sophie Allington, John Barber, Isabel Bowring, Trevor Boyer, Robert Gilmore, Rebecca Hardy, David Hurrell, Ian Jackson, Nicki Kemball, Steven Kirk, Rachel Lockwood, Malcolm McGregor, Dave Mead, Maurice Pledger, David Quinn, Chris Shields, Treve Tamblin, David Wright.

Usborne Publishing is not responsible and does not accept liability for the availability or content of any website other than its own, or for any exposure to harmful, offensive, or inaccurate material which may appear on the Web. Usborne Publishing will have no liability for any damage or loss caused by viruses that may be downloaded as a result of browsing the sites it recommends.